THE FEAR OF GOD

THE FEAR OF GOD
The Soul of Godliness

JOHN MURRAY

SOLID GROUND CHRISTIAN BOOKS
BIRMINGHAM, ALABAMA USA

Solid Ground Christian Books
PO Box 660132
Vestavia Hills AL 35266
205-443-0311
sgcb@charter.net
www.solid-ground-books.com

THE FEAR OF GOD
The Soul of Godliness

John Murray (1898-1975)

Cover image is taken from Rembrandt's *The Feast of
Belshazzar* which the publisher was privileged to view
in London. The terror on the faces is the most powerful
message captured by the gifted artist.

Cover design by Borgo Design
Contact them at borgogirl@bellsouth.net

ISBN- 978-159925-152-3

John Murray and *The Fear of God*

John Murray was born in 1898 Badbea, in Sutherland county, Scotland. Coming from the long line of Scottish Presbyterianism, Murray was trained from a young age to know and to treasure the Bible and the doctrine it contains. He served in the British Army in the First World War and soon after the war's end took up studies in theology. He studied first at the University of Glasgow and then at Princeton Theological Seminary where he studied under such notables as J. Gresham Machen and Geerhardus Vos. In 1929 he was asked to teach systematic theology at Princeton and accepted on the condition that he would only have to teach a single year. His limited agreement was providential, for the next year many of the faculty members, in the face of the theological liberalism polluting Princeton, left to found Westminster Theological Seminary. Murray was soon encouraged to join the faculty at the new school and did so, teaching there until 1966.

He retired to his native Scotland where, at the ripe old age of 69, he married and soon became the father of two children. He died in 1975, leaving a rich legacy of orthodox theology and a life lived for the glory of God.

Murray had a very high view of writing and thus waited until after his 50th birthday to publish his first book on *Christian Baptism* in 1952. This was followed by his books *Divorce* (1953), *Redemption Accomplished and Applied* (1955), *Principles of Conduct* (1957), and his magnum opus *A Commentary on the Epistle to the Romans* (1968). After his death in 1975 a project began which has resulted in the publication of his *Collected Writings* in 4 volumes (1976-1983).

The genesis of this booklet goes back nearly 30 years to the first time I read the chapter at the conclusion of Murray's book on Christian ethics bearing the simple title *Principles of Conduct*. The chapter had a profound impact the first time it was read, and has continued to impress and influence over the last three decades. From the opening sentence the attentive reader will sense that he is entering holy ground.

Professor Murray, as he was lovingly called, leads us by the hand into hallowed territory as we explore the forgotten doctrine of the fear of God. Sadly and tragically the modern concept of God does not evoke the awe and reverence that is found on every page of our Bibles. A quick glance at the Scripture Index on pages 23 and 24 will prove that this doctrine is found from Genesis to Revelation. Murray refers to no less than 38 books in the Bible as he sets forth his case that "the fear of God is the soul of godliness."

As a Christian publisher it is a privilege and honor to introduce this material to a world in desperate need of the knowledge of God. The words of the Lord through the prophet Hosea are all too true of our day: "My people are destroyed for a lack of knowledge" (4:6). The words spoken a few verses earlier reveal the nature of the knowledge they lacked: "There is no faithfulness or kindness or knowledge of God in the land" (4:1). It is our hope and prayer that this booklet will be scattered throughout the world and the knowledge of God will grow as a result. In the words of that same prophet I invite you to pick up this material to read for the good of your never-dying soul. "So let us know, let us press on to know the LORD. His going forth is as certain as the dawn; and He will come to us like the rain, like the spring rain watering the earth" (6:3).

Michael Gaydosh
Solid Ground Christian Books

THE FEAR OF GOD
The Soul of Godliness

Professor John Murray

The fear of God is the soul of godliness. The emphasis of Scripture in both the Old Testament and the New requires no less significant a proposition. Whether it be in the form, "The fear of the Lord is the beginning of wisdom" (Proverbs 9:10; Psalm 111:10) or "The fear of the Lord is the beginning of knowledge" (Proverbs 1:7), we are advised that what the Scripture regards as knowledge or wisdom takes its inception from the apprehension and emotion which the fear of God connotes. If we are thinking of the notes of biblical piety none is more characteristic than the fear of the Lord. "Hast thou considered my servant Job? for there is none like him in the earth, a perfect and upright man, one that feareth God, and escheweth evil" (Job 1:8). It is this same protestation that is repeated when our attention is particularly drawn to his persevering faithfulness and integrity (Job 2:3)—"he still holdeth fast his integrity." It is unnecessary to cite the scores of occasions throughout the Old Testament in which the fear of the Lord appears as the mark of God's people and enjoined as the sum of piety. Lest we should think that the religion of the Old Testament is *in this respect* on a lower level, and that the New Testament rises above that which is represented by the fear of the Lord, we need but scan the New Testament to be relieved of any such misapprehension. We are soon given to see that the notion of God's fear is not irrelevant in that piety which is the efflorescence of Old Testament faith. In the Magnificat of Mary we read: "And his mercy is unto generations and generations of those who fear him" (Luke 1:50). Could anything be more decisive than the words of the apostles: "Having therefore these promises, beloved, let us cleanse ourselves from all filthiness of the flesh and spirit, perfecting holiness in the fear of God" (2 Corinthians 7:1); "And ye servants, be subject in all things to those who are your masters according to the flesh, not with eyeservice as men-pleasers, but in singleness of heart, fearing the Lord" (Colossians 3:22); "Honour all men, love the brotherhood, fear God, honour the king" (1 Peter 2:17)? And nothing could be more significant than that the fear of the Lord should be coupled with the comfort of the Holy Spirit as the characteristics of the New Testament church: "So the church . . . walking in the fear of the Lord and in the comfort of the Holy Spirit was multiplied" (Acts 9:31). We may not forget that of him who is the shoot out of the stock of Jesse and the branch out of his roots, who judges the poor with righteousness and decides with equity for the meek of the earth, the girdle of whose waist is righteousness and of whose loins the girdle is faithfulness, of him it is said, "And the Spirit of the Lord shall rest upon him, the Spirit of wisdom and understanding, the Spirit of counsel and might, the Spirit of knowledge and of the fear of the Lord; and his delight shall be in the fear of the Lord" (Isaiah 11:2,3). If he who was holy, harmless, undefiled, and separate from sinners was endued with the Spirit of the fear of the Lord, how can thought or feeling that is not conditioned by God's fear have any kinship with him who is the captain of our salvation and who has given us an example that we should follow in his steps? The church walks in the fear of the Lord because the Spirit of Christ indwells, fills, directs, and rests upon the church and the Spirit of Christ is the Spirit of the fear of the Lord.

That ethical integrity is grounded in and is the fruit of the fear of God scarcely needs to be demonstrated. The earliest overt reference to the fear of God (Genesis 20:11) shows that Abraham was well aware that the ethical standards which should regulate marital relationships would not be in evidence where the fear of God was absent. "Surely the fear of God is not in this place; and they will slay me for my wife's sake." There was more integrity in Abimelech than Abraham apparently expected. But Abraham's recognition that the absence of the fear of God produced an ethic other than that of integrity is in accord with the total witness of Scripture. "Thou shalt not curse the deaf, nor put a stumblingblock before the blind; but thou shalt fear thy God: I am the LORD" (Leviticus 19:14; cf. 25:17,36). "The fear of the LORD is to hate evil: pride, and arrogancy, and the evil way, and the perverse mouth do I hate" (Proverbs 8:13; cf. 16:6). And surely the psalmist and apostle put this beyond question when they find the explanation of the catalogue of the transgressions of the wicked in the fact that "there is no fear of God before their eyes" (Romans 3:18; cf. Psalm 36:1).

The relation of the fear of God to the keeping of the commandments of God is indicated by the 'Preacher' when he says, "Let us hear the conclusion of the whole matter: fear God and keep his commandments; for this is the whole duty of man" (Ecclesiastes 12:13). The most practical of mundane duties derive their inspiration and impetus from the fear of God (cf. 2 Samuel 23:3; Colossians 3:22). The highest reaches of sanctification are realized only in the fear of God (cf. 2 Corinthians 7:1).

This emphasis which Scripture places upon the fear of God evinces the bond that exists between religion and ethics. The fear of God is essentially a religious concept; it refers to the conception we entertain of God and the attitude of heart and mind that is ours by reason of that conception. Since the biblical ethic is grounded in and is the fruit of the fear of the Lord, we are apprised again that ethics has its source in religion and as our religion is so will be our ethic. This is to say also that what or whom we worship determines our behavior. *What then is the fear of God?*

♦♦♦♦♦♦♦♦♦♦♦♦♦♦♦♦♦♦♦♦

There are at least two obviously distinct senses in which the word 'fear' is used in the Scripture.[1] Frequently it refers to the *terror and dread* which we entertain when we are afraid of some person or thing or complex of circumstances. When we read, "This day I will begin to put the dread of thee and the fear of thee upon the nations that are under the whole heaven, who shall hear report of thee, and shall tremble, and be in anguish because of thee" (Deuteronomy 2:25), it is clear that the fear spoken of is that of being afraid, of terror and dread. Or again, "Egypt was glad when they departed: for the fear of them fell upon them" (Psalm 105:38); here the same meaning is apparent. But when we read, "Ye shall fear every man his mother and his father" (Leviticus 19:3) it is equally obvious that the meaning is not that of terror but of *veneration and honor* (*cf.* Joshua 4:14).

It is this distinction that must be taken into account in dealing with the diverse injunctions of Scripture. When the Lord says to Joshua, "Fear not, neither be thou dismayed" (Joshua 8:1), what is in view is the fear of the enemies of Israel and has the same force as had been expressed earlier in different language, "Be strong and of good courage; be not afraid, neither be thou dismayed: for the Lord thy God is with thee whithersoever thou goest" (Joshua 1:9). It is the same cardinal thought, the avoidance of unbelieving anxious dread, that is pressed upon Israel: "Fear thou not; for I am with thee: be not dismayed; for I am thy God" (Isaiah 41:10; *cf.* verses 13,14; 43:1,5; 44:2; 51:7; 54:4,14). The same is urged upon the disciples by our Lord, "Fear not, little flock; for it is your Father's good pleasure to give you the kingdom" (Luke 12:32) and again, "Fear not them which kill the body" (Matthew 10:28; *cf.* 10:31; Luke 12:7,32).

It would be unnecessary to adduce the evidence establishing so obvious a distinction were it not the case that these two meanings of 'fear' enter into the concept of the fear of God. There is the dread or terror of the Lord and there is the fear of reverential awe. There is the fear that consists in being afraid; it elicits anguish and terror. There is the fear of reverence; it elicits confidence and love. Scripture introduces us to the former when we read of Adam after his fall: "And he said, I heard thy voice in the garden, and I was afraid because I was naked, and I hid myself" (Genesis 3:10). Our moral and spiritual sensitivities are seared if we do not sense the religious catastrophe which this reply of Adam demonstrates. Made for communion with God, he now flees from His presence because he is afraid. And this dread of the presence of God is the reason of his consciousness to the rupture which his sin had effected. Adam was afraid of God.

There is much loose thinking on this aspect of the question. Is it proper to be afraid of God? The only proper answer is that it is the essence of impiety not to be afraid of God when there is *reason* to be afraid. Adam's sin and his sin alone was the reason for the emotion of terror with which his soul had become stricken. But once he sinned the absence of this dread would have shown complete insensitivity to the revolution in which his sin consisted and which it also caused. For Adam to have behaved as if the rupture had not taken place would have been an unspeakable aggravation of his offence.

The Scripture throughout prescribes the necessity of this fear of God under all the circumstances in which our sinful situation makes us liable to God's righteous judgment. The person who did presumptuously in Israel and did not hearken to the priest who ministered in God's name was to be put to death, and we read, "And all the people shall hear, and fear, and do no more presumptuously" (Deuteronomy 17:13). The stubborn and rebellious son, a glutton and a drunkard, was to be stoned to death, and in this connection we read, "And all Israel shall hear and fear" (Deuteronomy 21:21). We must believe that in these contexts the fear mentioned is, principally at least, the fear evoked by the extreme punishment meted out to the transgressors involved, and the implication is that others would take warning from these examples and be inhibited from the commission of like offences by fear of the penalty. Again, lest we should think that this reflects a low plane of morality and motivation, worthy of the Old Testament but not of the gospel, we find this same kind of appeal in the New Testament itself. Nothing is more pertinent than our Lord's word, "Be not afraid of them who kill the body, but are not able to kill the soul: but rather be afraid of him who is able to destroy both soul and body in hell." (Matthew 10:28; *cf.* Luke 12:4,5). Jesus is pleading the necessity of that kind of fear which arises from the consideration of the judgment which God executes in the place of woe. It is futile to attempt to eliminate from the fear enjoined the terror which the thought of the final judgment of God is calculated to arouse. The writer of the Epistle to the Hebrews urges the fear of coming short as the incentive to diligence and perseverance. "Let us fear therefore, lest by any means, a promise being left of entering into his rest, any one of you should seem to come short of it" (Hebrews 4:1). And the same writer is not loath to bring the fearful expectation of judgment and the fierceness of the fire of God's vengeance, as the issues of apostasy, to bear upon the necessity of undeviating faith (Hebrews 10:27). He brings the warning to a conclusion by reminding us that "it is a fearful thing to fall into the hands of the living God" (verse 31).

The God of Scripture is holy and because he is holy his wrath rests upon sin. The strongest terms are enlisted to express the intensity of his indignation (*cf.* Exodus 15:7; Numbers 25:4; Isaiah 42:25; 51:17,20,22: 63:6; Jeremiah 4:8; 6:11; 42:18; Jonah 3:9; Nahum 1:6; Romans 2:9; 2 Thessalonians 1;8,9; Revelation 20:10,14,15). That those who are subject to this wrath should not dread it would be totally unnatural. It would be a violation of the infirmity inherent in our finitude not to be filled with horror and anguish at the thought of being subject to the fury of God's displeasure. Only the ignorant and hard-hearted could be destitute of this terror. And to aver that the fear of God's wrath and of the judgments which execute his wrath is an improper motive to action is to go counter to all that sound reason would dictate. Once we are convinced of the reality of God's judgment our hearts must react with terror and to be content to contain that terror violates human psychology. Why do we resist the thought of God's wrath? Why do we try to suppress the conviction of its reality? Is it not because we do not wish to entertain the terror which the conviction involves and we do not wish to be placed under the necessity of fashioning thought and life in terms of this reality? And if we cannot resist or suppress the conviction, are we no compelled in the nature of the case to think and act in terms of the reality of which we are convinced? But whatever may be true in the realm of human psychology, it is quite obvious that the Scripture represents the dread or terror of God's wrath as belonging to the total concept of the fear of God. Even where there is no sin, and therefore no

9

existent wrath, we cannot eliminate the fear of incurring God's displeasure as one motive deterrent to the commission of sin. We may not forget that the penal consequence of transgression was set forth to Adam before he fell: "In the day thou eatest thereof thou shalt surely die" (Genesis 2:17). And the same is adduced as a reason why he should not transgress. This is just to say that the fear of the consequence should have acted as a motive to deter him from sin. And shall we not say that the fear of incurring the displeasure of the Almighty is a motive in the ministry of the angels who have never sinned and have kept their first estate?

These foregoing considerations may help us to understand how this kind of fear is a necessity in the heart and life of the people of God. We should not be surprised when the psalmist proclaims: "My flesh trembleth for fear of thee; and I am afraid of thy judgements" (Psalm 119:120). It is the same piety of which Psalm 119 is redolent that could protest: "The Lord is my light and my salvation; whom shall I fear? The Lord is the strength of my life; of whom shall I be afraid?" (Psalm 27:1); "I will not be afraid of ten thousands of the people that have set themselves against me round about" (Psalm 3:6). Yet there is trembling and fear in the presence of God and of his judgments. The saint of God is not free from sin. He knows that sin is displeasing to God and he is keenly sensitive to the demands and judgments of his holiness. It is within this frame of thought and of feeling that we shall have to interpret those New Testament injunctions which never cease to have relevance to the believer during his sojourn here: "Work out your own salvation with fear and trembling; for it is God who worketh in you both to will and to do of his good pleasure" (Philippians 2:12,13); "And if ye call on the Father who without respect of persons judgeth according to each man's work, pass the time of you sojourning in fear" (1 Peter 1:17); "Be not high-minded, but fear; for if God spared not the natural branches, neither will he spare thee" (Romans 11:20,21). Humility, contrition, lowliness of mind are of the essence of godliness. And the dispositional complex which is characterized by these fruits of the Spirit is one that must embrace the fear and trembling which reflect our consciousness of sin and frailty. [If Peter had feared and trembled by reason of his own frailty, he would not have indulged in the protestation that though all would be offended yet would not he (*cf.* Matthew 26:31-35; Mark 14:27-31).] The piety of the New Testament is totally alien to the presumption of the person who is a stranger to the contrite heart and it is alien to the confidence of the person who never takes account of the holy and just judgments of God. The piety of the Bible is that of the contrite and humble spirit that trembles at God's Word (Isaiah 66:2). "Blessed are the poor in spirit: for theirs is the kingdom of heaven. Blessed are they that mourn: for they shall be comforted. Blessed are the meek: for they shall inherit the earth" (Matthew 5:3-5).

The fear of God which is the soul of godliness does not consist, however, in the dread which is produced by the apprehension of God's wrath. When the reason for such dread exists, then to be destitute of it is the sign of hardened ungodliness. But the fear of God which is the basis of godliness, and in which godliness may be said to consist, is much more inclusive and determinative than the fear of God's judgment. And we must remember that the dread of judgment will never of itself generate within us the love of God or hatred of the sin that makes us liable to his wrath. Even the infliction of wrath will not create the hatred of sin; it will incite to greater love of sin and enmity against God. Punishment has of itself no regenerating or converting power. The fear of God in which godliness consists is the fear which constrains adoration and love. It is the fear which consists in awe, reverence, honor, and worship, and all of these on the highest level of exercise. It is the reflex in our consciousness of the transcendent majesty and holiness of God. It belongs to all created rational beings and does not take its origin from sin. The essence of sin may be said to be negation of God's fear. Perhaps the most eloquent example of this fear of God is the adoration of the angelic host in Isaiah's vision. "In the year that King Uzziah died I saw the Lord sitting upon a throne, high and lifted up; and his train filled the temple. Above him stood the seraphim: each one had six wings; with twain he covered his face, and with twain he covered his feet, and with twain he did fly. And one cried unto another and said, Holy, holy, holy,

Angels do not fear God because of their sin.

Summary pt

is the Lord of hosts: the whole earth is full of his glory" (Isaiah 6:1-3). The reaction of the prophet is likewise significant. The angelic host is overwhelmed with awe and reverence before the manifestation of God's transcendent holiness. But there is no abashment because of their sin. It is otherwise with Isaiah. "Woe is me! for I am undone; because I am a man of unclean lips, and dwell in the midst of a people of unclean lips: for mine eyes have seen the King, the Lord of hosts" (verse 5). We have therefore the awe and adoration which the majesty of God must elicit from all rational creatures and we have also the complexion which the fact of our sinfulness must impart to that reverence and adoration.

◆◆◆◆◆◆◆◆◆◆◆◆◆◆◆◆◆◆◆

It is this fear of God that Scripture has in view when it reiterates throughout, "Thou shalt fear the Lord thy God" (Deuteronomy 6:13; 10:20). The controlling sense of the majesty and holiness of God and the profound reverence which this apprehension elicits constitute the essence of the fear of God. When we attempt to analyze this fear there are various elements or, at least, corollaries. There is the all-pervasive sense of the presence of God. "Whither shall I go from thy Spirit? Or whither shall I flee from thy presence? If I ascend up into heaven, thou art there: if I make my bed in Sheol, behold, thou art there. If I take the wings of the morning, and dwell in the uttermost part of the sea, even there shall thy hand lead me, and thy right hand shall hold me" (Psalm 139:7-10). And there is the all-pervasive sense of our dependence upon him and responsibility to him (*cf.* Psalm 139:1-6, 13-16, 23, 24; Acts 17:26-28; Romans 11:36; 1 Corinthians 8:6; Hebrews 2:10; Revelation 4:11). The fear of God implies our constant consciousness of relation to God, that, while we are also related to angels, demons, men, and things, our primary relationship is to God and all other relationships are determined by, and to be interpreted in terms of, our relation to him. The fool says in his heart "there is no God" and God is not in all the thoughts of the wicked (*cf.* Psalm 14:1; 10:4). The first thought of the godly man in every circumstance is God's relation to him and it, and his and its relation to God. That is God-consciousness and that is what the fear of God entails.

The Scripture graphically portrays the life of godliness in these terms. "And Enoch walked with God after he begat Methuselah three hundred years, and begat sons and daughters. . . and Enoch walked with God: and he was not, for God took him" (Genesis 5:22,24; *cf.* 6:9). "And when Abraham was ninety years old and nine, the Lord appeared to Abraham and said unto him, I am God Almighty; walk before me, and be thou perfect" (Genesis 17:1). The variation in the terms is likely intended to express the distinct facets of what is involved. Enoch walked with God and this, anthropomorphically, indicates his awareness of the presence of God and communion with him. Abraham is charged to walk before God and his life is represented as one lived in the constant consciousness of the inspection and direction of God. The anthropomorphism in the latter case points to the awe and circumspection which the knowledge of God's presence evokes, in the former case to the tenderness and intimacy of communion with God. These elements are correlative. That Abraham also walked with God and that he was distinguished by that trait, just as Enoch and Noah were, is apparent. He bears the distinction of being called the friend of God (2 Chronicles 20:7; Isaiah 41:8; James 2:23; *cf.* Genesis 18:17-19).

The relation of the fear of God to ethics appears in the case of Abraham most conspicuously. We marvel at the magnitude of Abraham's character. His magnanimity: "And Abraham said unto Lot, Let there be no strife, I pray thee, between me and thee, and between my herdsmen and thy herdsmen; for we are brethren. Is not the whole land before thee? separate thyself, I pray thee, from me: if thou wilt take the left hand, then I will go to the right; or if thou wilt take the right hand, then I will go to the left" (Genesis 13:8,9). And though higher considerations than those of magnanimity prompted his reply to the king of Sodom, yet these higher sanctions could not have found a place unless magnanimity had controlled his heart: "I have lifted up my hand unto the Lord, God Most High, possessor of heaven and earth, that I will not take a thread nor a shoe-latchet nor aught that is thine, lest thou shouldest say, I have made Abraham rich" (Genesis 14:22,23). Yet there is an amazing example of the sense of justice in this same incident. "Aner, Eshcol, and Mamre; let them have their portion" (verse 24). Magnanimity may constrain us to resign our own rights but never may it operate to deprive others of theirs - "let them have their portion". We think also of Abraham's filial loyalty: "And when Abram heard that his brother was taken, he led forth his trained men, born in his house, three hundred and eighteen, and pursued as far as Dan" (Genesis 14:14); "Cast out this handmaid and her son. . . And the thing was very grievous in Abraham's sight because of his son" (Genesis 21:10,11). And what is the secret of Abraham's nobility? The story informs us.

Obedience is the principle and secret of integrity. Next to his faith in God's promise, instant obedience to the commandment of God is the outstanding feature of Abraham's witness (*cf.* James 2:21,22). "Take now thy son, thine only son Isaac, whom thou lovest, and get thee into the land of Moriah; and offer him there for a burnt offering" (Genesis 22:2). The will of God was plain. Abraham did not hesitate. He rose early in the morning and set off to fulfill the command. The time for prayer was past, except the prayer for sustained strength of resolution. How different from Balaam who loved the wages of unrighteousness! And what is the Lord's word to Abraham? "And the angel of the Lord. . . said, Lay not thy hand upon the lad, neither do thou anything unto him; for now I know that thou fearest God, seeing thou hast

not withheld thy son, thine only son, from me"
(Genesis 22:11,12). The inferences are obvious.
God was proving Abraham and proving him in
respect of his fear of God. Abraham's
obedience demonstrated his fear of God. It was
because Abraham feared the Lord that he obeyed
God's voice. *God calls us to crucify the old man,*

The same relationship can be traced in the other
virtues that adorned Abraham's character. Why
could he have been so magnanimous to Lot? It
was because he feared the Lord and trusted his
promise and his providence. He had no need to
be mean; he feared and trusted the Lord. Why
could he have been magnanimous to the King of
Sodom? It was because he feared the Lord, God
Most High, possessor of heaven and earth, and
might not allow the enrichment offered to
prejudice the independence of his faith; he
needed not to be graspingly acquisitive. He could
offer up his son to whom the covenant promises
were attached because he feared the Lord. It all
amounts to this that nothing had value or
meaning for Abraham except in terms of his
relationship to God and God's to him, a
relationship focused in covenant promise and
faithfulness. *That* is all-pervasive God-
consciousness, and it is God-consciousness
conditioned by covenant-consciousness. This is
the fear of God or its indispensable corollary.

The character of Isaac has been underestimated
and sometimes he has been maligned.
Inspiration, however, has accorded Isaac a

How does God's covenant promise of faithfulness motivate me?

unique tribute. It has inscribed on its record the most unusual title as applied to God, one which is derived from the fear of God which Jacob had witnessed in his father Isaac. That Jacob recognized his father as sharing the faith of his grandfather Abraham is apparent. "O God of my father Abraham, and God of my father Isaac, O Lord, who saidst unto me, Return to thy country, and to thy kindred, and I will do thee good: I am not worthy of all the lovingkindness, and of all the truth, which thou hast showed unto thy servant; for with my staff I passed over this Jordan, and now I have become two bands" (Genesis 32:9,10). The humility, gratitude, and the faith of Jacob are nowhere illustrated more clearly than in this prayer, and the place of Isaac in the legacy of faith which provided the background of Jacob's own faith is hereby certified. But the distinctive tribute to the godliness of Isaac resides in that title by which on two previous occasions the God of Abraham and Isaac had been identified. "Except the God of my father, the God of Abraham, and the Fear of Isaac, had been with me, surely now hadst thou sent me away empty" (Genesis 31:42). "The God of Abraham, and the God of Nahor, the God of their father, judge betwixt us. And Jacob sware by the Fear of his father Isaac" (verse 53).

"The Fear of Isaac", as a name of God, witnesses to the profound and lasting impression produced upon Jacob by the fear of God which Isaac exhibited; it witnesses to the reality, depth, and pervasiveness of Isaac's godly fear; it shows that

Jacob's conception of the living God had been fashioned in terms of that which Isaac's fear implied; it constitutes on the part of Scripture a unique tribute to the place which the fear of God occupies in the thought and life of Isaac. The only explanation of Jacob's use of such a title is that Isaac's demeanor and behavior bespoke the profound sense of the majesty of God with which he was imbued.

◆◆◆◆◆◆◆◆◆◆◆◆◆◆◆◆◆◆

It is symptomatic of the extent to which the concept of the fear of God and the attitude of heart and mind which it represents has suffered eclipse that we have become reluctant to distinguish the earnest and consistent believer as 'God-fearing'. Perhaps our reluctance arises from the fact that believers manifest so little of the fear of God that we scarcely dare to characterize them as God-fearing; we may even be hesitant to call them godly. But whatever the reason, the eclipse of the fear of God, whether viewed as doctrinal or as attitude, evidences the deterioration of faith in the living God. Biblical faith means the fear of God, because the only God is "glorious in holiness, fearful in praises, doing wonders" (Exodus 15:11) and his name is glorious and fearful (*cf.* Deuteronomy 28:58). If we know God we must know him in the matchless glory of his transcendent majesty, and the only appropriate posture for us is prostration before him in awe and reverence. To think otherwise is to deny the transcendent greatness of God, and that is infidelity. The pervasive emphasis of Scripture upon the fear of God as the determinative attitude of heart in both religion and ethics and as the characteristic mark of God's people is exactly what must have been if the Bible is consistent with itself. The doctrine of God could know nothing else. To discount this emphasis and have any other is proof that the faith of the Bible is not ours. Our consciousness is not biblical unless it is conditioned by the fear of God.

The fear of God is the beginning of wisdom, and the perfection of glory in the world to come will only intensify its exercise. "Perfect love casts out fear" (1 John 4:18) but it is the fear of torment, not that of reverence and adoration. "Great and marvellous are thy works, Lord God Almighty; just and true are thy ways, O King of the nations: who shall not fear, O Lord, and glorify thy name? for thou only art holy; for all the nations shall come and worship before thee, for thy righteous acts have been made manifest" (Revelation 15:3,4). God's dread majesty can never be dissolved and neither can the sense of it in those who serve him. The deeper the apprehension of God's glory the more enhanced will be our wonderment. It will not be the wonderment of perplexity or horror but of reverential and exultant adoration.

The fear of God could be nothing less than the soul of rectitude. It is the apprehension of God's glory that constrains the fear of his name. It is that same glory that commands our totality commitment to him, totality trust and obedience.

The fear of God is but the reflex in our consciousness of the transcendent perfection which alone could warrant and demand the totality of our commitment in love and devotion. "Thou shalt love the Lord thy God with all thy heart, and with all thy soul, and with all thy mind, and with all thy strength" (Mark 12:30). It is the transcendent perfection of God, the fact that he is God and there is none else, that validates this totality demand. The fear of God in us is that frame of heart and mind which reflects our apprehension of who and what God is, and who and what God is will tolerate nothing less than totality commitment to him. The commandments of God are the concrete expressions to us of God's glory and will. If we are committed to him in devotion and love, we shall love his commandments, too. The fear of God and the love of God are but different aspects of our response to him in the glory of his majesty and holiness (*cf.* Deuteronomy 6:2,5,13). "The fear of the Lord is clean, enduring for ever: the judgments of the Lord are true and righteous altogether. More to be desired are they than gold, yea, than much fine gold: sweeter also than honey and the honeycomb. Moreover by them is thy servant warned: and in keeping them there is great reward" (Psalm 19:9-11).

ENDNOTE (from page 5)

[1] In Hebrew the notion of 'fear' is expressed usually by the two roots *yirah* and *pachad.* The former is used of the fear of God most frequently and does service for both senses in which we may fear God: (1) the fear of being afraid of God and his punitive judgments; (2) the fear of reverential awe and adoration. To express the latter the root *yirah* may be said to be the standard term. The instances of this meaning are so numerous that it is unnecessary to cite them. Of the former sense cf. Genesis 3:10; Exodus 3:6; Deuteronomy 5:5; 17:13; 19:20; 2 Samuel 6:9; Psalm 119:120; Jonah 1:16. We are not to think that these two meanings are antithetical or incompatible. The 'terribleness' of God, expressed by the Niphal Participle of *yirah* (cf. Exodus 15:11; Deuteronomy 7:21; 10:17; 28:58 ; 1 Chronicles 16:25; Nehemiah 1:5; Psalm 47:2; 111:9; Daniel 9:4; Malachi 1:14), is that which demands awe, and it excites terror in all who are subject to the judgments of his holy indignation. Deliverance from this terror is the fruit of God's propitiatory grace. Exodus 20:20 is an interesting example of exhortation to put away the fear of terror and to entertain the fear of reverence and obedience.

The root *pachad* bears more frequently the meaning of being afraid, of terror (cf. Exodus 15:16; Job 3:25; Isaiah 33:14; 51:13; Micah 7:17). But that *pachad* can be used for reverential awe is apparent from the following instances: Genesis 31:42,53; Psalm 36:1; 119:120,161; Jeremiah 2:19; Hosea 3:5. It is difficult to determine the precise shade of meaning in Proverbs 28:14, but it is probable that the fear of coming short of God's commandments and of falling into sin is in the foreground. In any case the fear in view is commended. Isaiah 60:5 is an interesting example of the use of *pachad* in the sense of joyful emotion. Apparently the thought is that the heart throbs with pleasure.

In the New Testament the terms generally used to express fear are *phobos* and *phobeo.* They are used very frequently to express the idea of being afraid. In the sense of the fear that we owe to God these terms occur (cf. Matthew 10:28; Luke 1:50; 23:40; Acts 9:31; Romans 3:18; 11:20; 2 Corinthians 7:1; Colossians 3:22; Revelation 14:7; 15:4). They are also used with reference to the fear and trembling which are enjoined upon us in the path of obedience and perseverance (cf. 1 Corinthians 2:3; Ephesians 6:5; Philippians 2:12; Hebrews 4:1).

Scripture Index

Scripture Index

PRINCIPLES OF CONDUCT
Aspects of Biblical Ethics
John Murray

A modern theological classic, John Murray's *Principles of Conduct* clearly shows the organic unity and continuity of the biblical ethic. Murray here addresses ethical questions relating to such topics as marriage, labor, capital punishment, truthfulness, Jesus' teaching in the Sermon on the Mount, law and grace and the fear of God (as seen in this booklet). Though the Ten Commandments furnish the core of the biblical ethic, Murray points the reader again and again to all of Scripture as the basic and final authority in all matters of Christian conduct.

J.I. Packer wrote in the Foreword, "An inheritor of the combined wisdom of Puritanism and Princeton, Murray did his work as a trustee of the Reformed tradition. . . . His special contribution was to buttress and burnish this heritage through the discipline of biblical theology, practiced according to the redemptive-historical approach that the great Geerhardus Vos, one of Murray's teachers, pioneered a century ago."

If you have been struck to the heart by reading *The Fear of God* you will want to acquire and devour *Principles of Conduct,* the book from which this material has been extracted.

ISBN: 978-0-8028-1144-8

Principles of Conduct may be purchased from Wm. B. Eerdmans Publishing Company by calling 800-253-7521, or sending an email to customerservice@eerdmans.com.

OTHER SOLID GROUND TITLES

We recently celebrated our seventh anniversary of uncovering buried treasure to the glory of God. During these seven years we have produced nearly 200 volumes. A sample is listed below:

Biblical & Theological Studies: *Addresses to Commemorate the 100th Anniversary of Princeton Theological Seminary in 1912* by Allis, Machen, Wilson, Vos, Warfield and many more.

Notes on Galatians by J. Gresham Machen

The Origin of Paul's Religion by J. Gresham Machen

A Scientific Investigation of the Old Testament by R.D. Wilson

Theology on Fire: *Sermons from Joseph A. Alexander*

Evangelical Truth: *Sermons for the Family* by Archibald Alexander

A Shepherd's Heart: *Pastoral Sermons of James W. Alexander*

Grace & Glory: *Sermons from Princeton Chapel* by Geerhardus Vos

The Lord of Glory by Benjamin B. Warfield

The Person & Work of the Holy Spirit by Benjamin B. Warfield

The Power of God unto Salvation by Benjamin B. Warfield

Calvin Memorial Addresses by Warfield, Johnson, Orr, Webb...

The Five Points of Calvinism by Robert Lewis Dabney

Annals of the American Presbyterian Pulpit by W.B. Sprague

The Word & Prayer: *Classic Devotions from the Pen of John Calvin*

A Body of Divinity: *Sum and Substance of Christian Doctrine* by Ussher

The Collected Works of James H. Thornwell

A Puritan New Testament Commentary by John Trapp

Exposition of the Epistle to the Hebrews by William Gouge

Exposition of the Epistle of Jude by William Jenkyn

Lectures on the Book of Esther by Thomas M'Crie

Lectures on the Book of Acts by John Dick

To order any of our titles please contact us in one of three ways:

Call us at **1-866-789-7423**
Email us at **sgcb@charter.net**
Visit our website at **www.solid-ground-books.com**